Photo credit: Andy Baker

Jane Hutcheon is a journalist, author and former China correspondent who's reported from some of the most volatile, exotic and fascinating places on Earth. She wrote and performed *Lost in Shanghai* which premièred at the 2022 Sydney Festival. From 2010-2019 she was creator and host of ABCTV's One Plus One conducting in-depth conversations with more than 500 celebrities, authors, thinkers and everyday heroes. She's written several books. Her latest book is *Rebel Talk: the art of powerful conversations.*

ISBN 9781922598134 (print)
ISBN 9781922598943 (ebook)

Published in Australia and New Zealand by:

Brio Books, an imprint of Booktopia Group Ltd
Unit E1, 3-29 Birnie Avenue
Lidcombe, NSW 2141, Australia
briobooks.com.au

Printed and bound in Australia by Ligare

booktopia.com.au

Rebel Talk

Jane Hutcheon

Author's Note

Unless otherwise stated, quotes from *One Plus One* interviews have been taken from show transcripts and lightly edited for clarity. Permission to use the transcripts was granted by ABC News.

For Isla

Contents

Foreword by

Sir David Suchet CBE

I first met Jane in Sydney in 2014 when I performed in the *Last Confession* playing the role of Cardinal Benelli. I was invited to appear on Jane's *One Plus One* show. I was told what the show was all about and I looked forward to meeting her because I had watched a little bit of her work beforehand. In all honesty, it came as an extremely lovely surprise to meet someone who was genuinely interested in asking me questions and listening to my replies.

Jane is a wonderful listener. She's extremely engaging and immediately makes you feel like her friend. She's very warm, she's very open and she's very giving in her style of interviewing.

What she brought to *One Plus One*, as far as I was concerned, was a genuine warmth, humility and curiosity. I felt very welcome. And anybody who has been interviewed by her, I'm sure will have felt the same.

When theatre producer Liza McLean came to me with the idea of doing a show: *David Suchet* – Poirot *and More, a Retrospective*, we discussed it and thought, rather than just doing a one-man show, it would be great to have someone in the chair interviewing me and sharing the evening with me. Immediately, without even a question, I remembered my interview with Jane and I said, 'I want Jane Hutcheon please.'

The producer turned around and exclaimed, 'That's exactly who I would have chosen as well!'

And I replied, 'Well, please invite her.'

I am the most fortunate of actors to have had Jane sharing the stage with me as we travelled through Australia and New Zealand in January and February 2020 in twenty-one theatre shows. It's an experience we won't forget.

I'm absolutely delighted she's now sharing some of her observations and secrets about the craft of conversation, listening and interviewing in this book, *Rebel Talk*.

Introduction

Have you ever tried slicing the top off a soft-boiled egg? The eggshell splinters and separates. It never looks as neat as you intended and the yolk starts to drip over the edge. It's a bit like that when a conversation goes wrong; it's unpredictable and messy. We can't control the direction of the conversation or the outcome. We can, however, accept our shortcomings and learn from our mistakes. With a bit of reflection and practice, we can elevate our conversations to a new realm: solving complex problems, producing inspiring ideas, adding value and even preventing space-flight disasters. This is what I call, Rebel Talk.

As a professional conversationalist – aka journalist – I've been striking up conversations for more than 30 years. My estimate is, over my career, I've conducted somewhere in the region of 10,000 interviews. Journalism perfectly satisfied my restless curiosity; my need to be nosey. I've been fortunate to have spoken with people from all walks of life and from many corners of the Earth, from a shepherd watching his flock on the wintry slopes of Bethlehem, to an exorcist exhibiting the shackles embedded in a cell in the Vatican. I have relished my licence to ask questions, then as now.

From 2010, my conversations became more structured. I developed and hosted a weekly interview show called *One Plus One* on ABC Television. Over nine years I conducted more than 500 face-to-face, in-depth conversations, using questions to draw out the masterpieces and misery, triumphs and setbacks, the ebb and flow of my guests' lives. The 30-minute show featured celebrities, writers, actors and scientists as well as many little-known heroes.

Communication has always been a rich and exciting backdrop to my life. I grew up in Hong Kong where my parents were journalists. My dad eventually became a newspaper editor. Our family of five, plus a big black dog, lived on the eighth floor of an apartment building. When a Canadian family moved into a unit below us, I started bucket-mailing one of the daughters, sending questions scrawled on scraps of paper, placed in a bucket and lowered on a piece of string with a bell attached to signal that a message had arrived.

Eventually my friend and I grew tired of the game and the bucket dangled empty like a telephone left off the hook. Something new had come along. Not long after bucket-mail, my parents brought home a Texas Instruments computer that they hooked up to the TV set. This, we were told, was the future. My brothers and I stared at the flashing cursor, wondering what magic might appear if only we could master BASIC, the computer programming language.

Back then I couldn't have imagined that later I would carry a much more powerful computer in my pocket. From bucket-mail to iPhone, the communications revolution of the last fifty years has transformed how we live and work. It's made the world a much smaller, more accessible place too. I witnessed this working as an international correspondent in China, the Middle East and Europe from 1995–2008 and after that as a news presenter. From a studio the size of a cupboard in Sydney you can cover news breaking in Scandinavia. Humanity is unrelentingly connected. Many of our conversations today take place on smart devices. Banking, paying bills, booking appointments, reporting faults and online shopping are some of the transactions we undertake that don't require direct human contact. Yet despite this unparalleled level of connection, how much value do we still place in face-to-face communication? And are we gradually losing the ability to communicate?

In late 2019, a challenge emerged that is redefining how we communicate. COVID-19 began spreading around the world like a silent bushfire. In the summer of 2020, many tracts of Australia had been ravaged by fires but the creep of COVID turbocharged the sense of emergency. In late February 2020 I arrived home on what was to be my last international flight for the year. A month later, borders slammed shut. Venues such as restaurants, pubs, cinemas and gyms were closed as Australian infections and deaths mounted. Almost a million people lost their jobs. In the space of two days, my projects for the year were cancelled. The smoke from the bushfires had long dissipated but a sense of upheaval lingered.

The upheaval that upended the world wasn't all dismal. For instance, planes no longer flew over my house, which is under a flight path. In the silence, cackling kookaburras and bird calls replaced the rumble of jet engines, as if nature had been woken from a long slumber.

Australian and New Zealand researchers[1] discovered that the global slowdown in human activity cut the amount of seismic vibration we normally create by one-half. Scientists have dubbed the change 'the anthropause'. Most of us went through a personal anthropause too. I left my job as a TV interviewer in September 2019 and in March 2020 when all of my new projects were cancelled, I worried about the loss. Yet with so many people in the same boat (and many far worse off than me) I decided to swap a sense of despair for a sense of exploration. I began to research my new circumstances through a lens of curiosity. I'll fondly remember my anthropause as being a time of self-awareness and productivity.

Early one morning, I heard a familiar voice coming from the TV. Though it's ridiculous to say this, I didn't immediately recognise it as me. It turned out to be a replay of my show, which was broadcast five days a week before the morning news. I watched my interview with former dancer Eileen Kramer, who was 104 at the time of recording. She'd lived such a full, big life and on returning to Australia at the age of 100 she'd continued to choreograph and produce dance works. It was refreshing to watch the conversation from the perspective of a viewer, and I found myself completely focused on the conversation and the emotions it ignited. Then TV Jane said goodbye. My show ended and the news began. As in a deluge, bad news flooded my senses. In the early pandemic days, news became so addictive despite the shortage of real information. I watched until I realised, I'd had enough fear and calamity and returned regularly to the refuge of my TV conversations.

Around this time, I also watched an infamous video showing women fighting over toilet-paper in a suburban supermarket. A mother and daughter had managed to fill a shopping trolley with eight large packages of toilet-paper. After a brawl with a third woman who'd tried to grab one of the packages, the grabber says: 'I just want one pack.'

'No,' replies the trolley woman, 'Not one pack.'

This conversation stayed with me. In the early months of the pandemic, toilet-paper became something that seemed important for many of us to stockpile and it quickly disappeared from the supermarket shelves. The conversation between the brawling women was really about unspoken fear which triggered an angry response that became physical. Somebody had thought to video the event and the supermarket managers who came to restore order eventually called the police. I've often wondered whether the incident could have been resolved more amicably by the presence of an individual with the ability to calm nerves, lower the temperature of the argument and change the path of the conversation.

At moments like #toiletpapergate, what was needed was the voice of a peacemaker. Instead, the conversation ended up in court, wasting time, effort and resources.

At this point in our history we are at the intersection of a number of crises including controlling a pandemic, economic distress, disinformation, environmental degradation, inadequate safety nets, gender inequality and at times, government ineptitude. On an individual level, we feel numbness swirling around us like morning fog. The fog is a toxic cocktail that includes elements of fatigue, anxiety and stress. In short, we are in a state of burnout.

As I watched my old TV interviews, I started to ask myself, is the pandemic a catalyst to rethink how we communicate? Could we break through the numbness and discover how to talk like Rebels? Could we:

- transform poor conversation habits
- speak up about problems
- generate energy, passion and optimism

- look for opportunities
- stop lecturing and giving unsolicited advice
- learn the art of humble listening?

What the world needs is a dedicated band of conversation Rebels. By 'rebels', I don't mean troublemakers. I'm talking about people who are prepared to be a bit brave: to challenge and shake things up by researching, asking questions, listening and making informed choices to achieve better outcomes.

Fear, fatigue, anxiety and uncertainty are the emotional hallmarks of these times. We've reached a plateau. But here's the thing; despite periods of loss and hardship, many of us – including me – have found great contentment and a sense of purpose. Nearly one in two people say the pandemic has gifted them the time to reflect and they now have a greater sense of what is important.[2]

Conversation doesn't come easily to everybody. A third of us love to chat and will talk any time of the day on any subject.[3] But the remaining two-thirds of us are not chatty types. We find conversation challenging because of shyness, introversion, social anxiety, communication disabilities or learning difficulties or because we don't feel fluent or articulate. One in two people say they feel lonely at least once a week.[4] Our homes have become workplaces. Traditional jobs are disappearing. Routines have been broken, travel plans are on hold and protocols have been reinvented. We don't know when life will go back to normal and what a future 'normal' will look like.

In this climate, I'm particularly worried about three things:

- **Technology.** It is not a substitute for human connection. Remember when friendship and discussions with colleagues were conducted in person? We discussed ideas deep into the night instead of posting them on LinkedIn. We expressed our feelings in words instead of using 'thumbs up' emojis. The internet and social-media platforms leave many conversations half-finished and unsatisfying. As Twitter's co-founder Jack Dorsey told me, 'these (platforms) are tools, something that allow us to work faster, to work smarter, to help us reflect on what we're doing. They are meant to ideally make humans better.' While technology is a vehicle for people to communicate, I'd suggest what makes human beings better is thoughtful conversation rather than the filter of technology.

- **Polarisation.** More than two centuries ago, American founding father Alexander Hamilton lost a pistol duel to his political nemesis Aaron Burr. The duel resulted in Hamilton's untimely death, although thanks to a popular book which inspired a musical blockbuster, we know more about Hamilton than we might have known otherwise. Happily, the duel is a thing of the past but in politics it's apparent we have moved even further away from productive agreement and learning to bridge divides.

- **Selective listening.** This happens when we're focused on being right or we've already made up our minds about an issue, and we accept only the parts of a conversation that confirm our beliefs or intentions. It happens in workplaces and homes and in our governments and institutions.

Conversation is at the heart of our lives and this book is an invitation to re-examine your communication style, learn new skills and choose braver outcomes. Rebel talk is a tool I invented, distilled from more than thirty years of personal and professional conversations. This book will help you:

- get to the point
- understand and be understood
- approach difficult conversations
- strengthen relationships and networks
- be more assertive
- develop curiosity
- be kinder to yourself, and others as a result
- develop quality conversations.

'Almost all of us have some kind of communication problem that we don't know we have,' says actor and science-communicator Alan Alda. Yet most of us think we are pretty good at conversation and any problems belong to the *other* person.

While the education system teaches us writing and numbers (literacy and numeracy), few of us are ever taught the art of talking: oracy. We aren't trained how to understand another person or how to talk clearly. We aren't encouraged to challenge ourselves for our own benefit.[5] We aren't instructed how to share our opinions or disagree respectfully. Some of us are shamed for having the 'wrong opinion' and silenced because our views offend others. Former Paralympian (and one of my successors on *One Plus One*) Kurt Fearnley told me 'one of the things that is uniquely Australian is that we admire people who don't complain. You're a whinger if you complain.'

Are we a nation of loudmouths or are we just loud?[6] Where do you stand on the conversation ladder? Are you patient, compliant, un-complaining? Are you forgiving or do you hold grudges? Do you discuss differences with your friends or blank someone who hurts your feelings? Do you relish or run from confrontation? Do you value heart-felt apologies?

Rebel talk is more urgent than ever.

Chapter One

Why Rebel?

I once bought a car after convincing myself I was just going window-shopping. How, you might ask, did I manage that? Quite simply because the sales manager, Johanna, was excellent at her job. Instead of talking at me and my husband, she asked a series of relevant questions:

> What will you mostly use the car for?
>
> Do you plan to take long-distance trips?
>
> What features in a car are important to you?
>
> How many people do you need to transport?
>
> How much storage space will you need?

We had our eye on one of the vehicles, a bit fancier than our station wagon. 'It's a great car,' I said but I don't think it will fit in our carport.' I actually LOVED that car.

Then came the game-changing question. 'Why don't you drive it home and see if it fits in the space?'

I drove it home. It was an amazingly comfortable ride. The car did fit into our carport. That was four years ago now.

We own that car in large part due to Johanna's listening skills.

I recently got back in touch with Johanna to ask her about where she learned her craft. She had moved companies but was still dedicated to selling cars. Johanna says she enjoys helping people. 'I see my job as a matchmaker, the right person with the right vehicle. I used to be a wedding planner and I would say back then that I was part of the best day of people's lives. Now, selling cars, I'm responsible for *many* best days of people's lives. It's a privilege to get to share that moment.'

Surprisingly, many people who work with customers neglect to do what Johanna does instinctively: they don't ask good questions and they don't listen to the replies. Further up the chain of command, conversations go wrong and leaders don't listen. Billions of dollars are spent trying to repair or cover-up communication failures. One government enterprise hired a $3,000-a-day reputation consultant to fix its image after cutting services. In some cases, miscommunication can have tragic consequences.

Chris Hadfield is a former NASA astronaut and the first Canadian to command the International Space Station. He became famous after a video-clip he made went viral. It was of Chris singing a version of David Bowie's *Space Oddity* while on the International Space Station. The clip's been viewed about fifty million times.

When I interviewed Chris, we discussed the 2003 tragedy of space shuttle *Columbia* when seven astronauts died. Chris had known all of them. As an astronaut, experienced pilot, test-pilot and engineer, Chris was trained to look out for 'the next thing that was going to kill me.' On launch day at the Kennedy Space Center in January 2003 Chris said, 'We all knew *Columbia* was damaged during launch.' A recording from one of the ground cameras showed a piece of insulation foam from the external fuel tank peeling off and hitting the shuttle's wing during lift-off. Chris reckoned he had watched the video a hundred times. 'That's not what normally happens,' he said.

'But even with my standing in the agency – I'd flown in space twice – the voice that I had within NASA and the world space program, I looked at that (video) and I said "That's not what we normally see. But everyone thinks it's okay. I'm just going to live with it. I think it's okay too."'

Sixteen days later during the shuttle's return to Earth, Chris watched *Columbia* break-up and disintegrate across the Texas sky. It was a gut-wrenching moment. 'I felt a huge sense of emotional loss and a sense of culpability. I saw that we (NASA) had done something wrong,' he admitted. 'I could have been the person within the organisation that stood up and said, "Look, I know everybody thinks it's okay but we need to go look at that wing." You couldn't see the damaged part without going on a space-walk.'

In the middle of that shock and grief, a realisation came.

'We collectively killed those seven people by not doing everything we could. And I was just as guilty as anybody else within the whole organisation. I contributed to an amazingly public and horrifically violent death of friends of mine.'

Miscommunication, fear and poor listening all played a part in the disaster. Apart from human tragedy, the investigation and clean-up cost US$400 million.

If you've ever failed to speak up when something in your midst has gone horribly wrong, you are not alone.

Sometimes it's hard enough to simply show up. A few years ago, my boss invited me to an awards evening, which I was chuffed about, but it also combined all my apprehensions – wearing formal clothes, mingling with people I didn't know and being stuck next to executives with whom I have little or nothing in common. Even the lead-up to the event – finding a dress that wasn't going to send me broke – induced anxiety. As the taxi set me down at the venue, a grand art gallery, my stomach was so knotted I was tempted to ask the driver to turn around and drive me home.

It turns out I am far from being the only one to feel shy and self-conscious in social settings. Scientists, doctors, teachers, engineers, corporate leaders, stay-at-home parents; intelligent, accomplished people are among those who struggle in social situations. Many of us need help initiating and nurturing our conversations.

A few years ago, I saw a nutmeg fruit *Myristica fragrans* for the first time. It was growing in a spice plantation in Zanzibar. The kernel (the hard seed that we call nutmeg) is covered by a deep, red vein which, when removed, dried and ground, is known as mace. Nutmeg and mace are nothing without each other. They are intertwined like conversation and listening. I remember my delight when first witnessing this symbiotic relationship. When you discover that conversation is nothing without engaged listening it's hard to let go of this image of a nutmeg in its vibrant cocoon.

The 500 interviews I conducted for *One Plus One* provided me with an insight into how to craft conversations. I've tied together the key components of conversation using the acronym REBEL.

Readiness research and prepare

Empathy to connect and engage

Be curious ask questions

Engage attention humble listening

Lead the way choose how to respond

Once you've learned the skills behind each element of REBEL, you'll be able to put them into practice immediately. Whether negotiating with your boss or your teenager, getting the most out of your daily connection with people, having a difficult or awkward conversation with your partner or parent, these tips will give you a kernel of confidence in your own conversations.

Now, are you ready?

Chapter Two

Readiness

Before becoming a foreign correspondent and an interviewer, I presented a nightly business segment on TV. A highlight of the financial year was co-hosting the national budget, live in the studio.

I spent Budget Day with other journalists in a 'lock-up', reading through the government's embargoed budget papers, meaning you get to see the material in advance of the publication time. The big moment is the budget speech, delivered in the evening by the Federal Treasurer. A downside to the lock-up is that you have to stay in a secure location for most of the day. By the time I arrived back at the studio, I was full of adrenaline, clutching my scrawled notes, my jacket, an earpiece and a few pages of type-written script. As I pushed open the heavy studio door and took my chair, I felt on top of what I had to do. No worries.

The chief presenter, Paul, was in Canberra to interview senior politicians. I was in the Sydney studio with the main production team – the executive producer, supervising producer, studio director and an autocue operator. I expected the team to have everything under control. They had my back. We were professionals who'd been doing this for a while. All I had to do was read the autocue, ask some questions and hand over to our man in Canberra.

The coverage began well. I finished interviewing an economist and started to read the scripted commentary on autocue in front of me. If you've ever watched *The West Wing,* you've probably seen President Jed Bartlet reading off those small screens with words that scroll as he delivers his speech. That's what's known as 'autocue' and it's what television presenters use every day to deliver the news. About three minutes after I began to read my autocue the words just stopped. I stared at an empty black screen. In the dimly lit studio, I glanced nervously at the autocue operator metres away. Like a silent movie star, she mouthed the words 'no more'. Her eyes wide and dramatic, she shook her head in case I hadn't read her lips.

What the operator meant was that she'd run out of text. For whatever reason, the autocue scripts just couldn't be produced fast enough to keep up with the live broadcast. Then I heard the director's voice in my earpiece. 'Canberra is running late. The presenter's not ready. Can you fill (TV jargon meaning fill the time)? He's five minutes away.'

If you've ever tried to talk publicly for *two* minutes

let alone *five*, it feels like an eternity. But thanks to my misplaced confidence, I wasn't fazed. *No worries*, I thought again. *Big smile. I can fill.*

After running out of superficial budget-related recaps, I resorted to reading from my notebook but my handwriting was a mad mix of shorthand and scrawls. I kept tripping over my words. Then I re-read some old scripts from the desk in front of me, I told an anecdote about what budget day was like for journalists and I repeated the major points as far as I could remember them.

Through the earpiece, the director encouraged me, 'That's great! Keep going!' Eventually, after feeling like I'd entered a trance, the voice in my ear said, 'Okay, Paul's ready. We're going to Canberra now.'

I had been filling for more than ten minutes. Then there was one final insult.

I assumed that the audience by now was seeing my colleague Paul in Canberra. I flopped back into my chair, rolling my eyes and mouthed 'phew', only to discover that the camera had accidentally switched back to me and caught this indignity (aka blooper) mid eye-roll just in case the audience needed a last laugh.

Once safely off-air, the rims of my ears began to burn. The TV smile dissolved. I ripped off the lapel microphone and marched out of the studio with my boss, the executive producer, tearing behind me.

'We were a joke!' I barked and he didn't argue.

When I eventually got home and fell asleep that night, I dreamed that I resigned, over and over and over again. Fortunately, this all happened pre-social media. The pain receded long ago and I've dined out on that story more than a few times.

Why am I telling it to you? Because this particular embarrassment was about *not* being ready. What was I thinking going into budget night armed only with my reporter's notebook and a lot of hubris?

Now, you may not feel that you have to *research* your conversations, but a little *preparation* can be useful. In my case, more back-up scripts on the desk would have been a start. Having a guest with me at the presenter's desk would have been a good idea too.

I recall that it was the executive producer's first time overseeing a budget program and it was *my* first time being solo in the studio for such a big event.

If I had taken more time to **prepare and rehearse** the outcome could have been very different.

Try It Out

Ask yourself ... RIO

What **R**esources could help?

What's the **I**ntention of the conversation?

What's the desired **O**utcome?

If I'd asked myself these questions *before* Budget Night, here's what I might have said:

- **Resources:** scripts, extra staff, rehearsal or run-through
- **Intention:** my purpose is to present the budget in a clear and authoritative manner.
- **Outcome:** smooth delivery and clear communication.

Asking the RIO questions puts your head in the right space. It becomes clear what preparation you need, whether it's an extra producer to write the scripts to ensure they don't run out, a few simple notes (rather than reading from my scrawled reporter's notebook), a Plan B for when it goes pear-shaped.

Have a script

Have you ever scribbled notes on a napkin before a significant conversation? I carry sticky notes with me and make a list of pointers before conversations with teachers, doctors, salespeople and so on. I like to be prepared and it removes the anxiety of forgetting something important.

Practice 'yutori'

When I left my job as an interviewer, I visualised my perfect future; I wanted to lead a more 'deliberate' life. In other words, I wanted to choose projects that ignited my passion and interest. As I thought about the purpose behind the desire, I realised it was about how I wanted to spend time. Having a deliberate life was about being less rushed and more fulfilled.

After the Second World War, Japan's economy grew quickly until it reached 10% of the world's combined Gross National Product. In terms of the standard of living however, many Japanese felt their lives had been robbed of satisfaction and a sense of fulfilment. A common expression was 'no *yutori* can be found in our daily lives'. Officials set about trying to address this by incorporating 'yutori' which is living with spaciousness, elbowroom, latitude, breathing space, into a measurement of psychological well-being.

As it's quite a loose concept, here's how I apply yutori:

- arrive early at appointments/meetings instead of booking them back-to-back (this goes for Zoom meetings too)
- make notes to catch thoughts, feelings and ideas
- focus on what you are doing
- schedule time to connect with your friends, trusted colleagues and collaborators
- make your conversations deliberate
- take breaks to stand up, walk around and breathe
- restrict email correspondence to one or two blocks in a day.

Researchers from Queens University in Canada recently discovered that they could isolate 'thought worms', which is when a thought begins and ends.[7] Humans have more than 6000 thoughts a day, the researchers found. No wonder we feel so busy.

I love the idea of thoughts as worms wriggling through the mind. Mine would be glow worms. If we thought about gathering resources, intentions and outcomes for our important conversations, I wonder what effect that would have on the worm farms of our minds and how that might in turn transform our conversations?

Chapter Three

Empathy

In my final year studying journalism, our major assignment was to produce a half-hour radio documentary. I chose to do mine on the subject of people addicted to 'pokies', poker or gaming machines.

I contacted the local chapter of Gamblers Anonymous, which supports people trying to manage their addiction. The spokesman, Daryl, invited me to meet a group of individuals whom I never would have suspected were gambling addicts. Before long, they talked about what their gambling had cost them. As we sat together in a semi-circle, Daryl spoke emotionally about losing everything he valued: his job, his house, his wife and his children. He described his painful experience in vivid terms and I asked him whether he'd agree to talk to me for the assignment. Fortunately, he said yes.

Looking back now, my first in-depth interview reminds me of the privilege of journalism which gave me a passport to a lifetime of meaningful conversations. In the studio that day I began to ask Daryl the '5Ws 1H' formula: The *What, Why, When, Where, Who and How* questions journalists are trained to pose. I remember being taught that this should become like second nature to us.

Yet what unfolded in the studio was not about extracting information. What transpired was a discussion about humanity and courage, failure and vulnerability. It was about someone trusting me with their story. For the first time, I experienced what it was like to be a journalist; I felt a great sense of purpose and just a little bit powerful.

A bouncing red needle on the instrument panel in front of me confirmed the conversation was being recorded and my mind shifted between listening to Daryl and enjoying the experience of being the one asking questions. After several minutes, Daryl's volume started to drift lower as if he were telling me a secret. He wasn't looking at me anymore. He gazed at the console in front of him, hesitating.

He mumbled, 'That's when I tried to take my own life.'

Everything slowed down. My chest pounded. Daryl continued his story as I processed the candid detail he'd just shared with me. When I think back to what twenty-year-old Jane did next, it seems unbelievable now. What did I do? I interrupted him.

'Daryl?' I began, 'would you mind saying that last bit again?'

He paused. 'Which bit?'

'The part about when you tried to kill yourself. I'm going to ask you "What did you do then?" And could you say what you said with more emphasis please?'

He paused again, nodded and did exactly as I had requested.

After the assignment was graded and returned, I recall my supervisor saying something along the lines of how I hadn't handled Daryl with enough empathy. While young Jane didn't analyse it much at the time, I've often thought about this since. Young Jane was obsessed with the idea that she had to record something memorable: 'This is radio. What if listeners missed the significance of what he was saying because it wasn't expressed forcefully enough?'

Whatever Daryl really thought about my interjection, his reaction was one of generosity. Looking back now, I feel my insensitive behaviour didn't create a bond. I didn't build empathy. This is why people often criticise interviewers who constantly interrupt their guests. It breaks the empathy connection.

In real-life conversations, non-verbal behaviour such as Daryl's voice becoming quiet (and other gestures like a tone change, eye contact, body language, or physiological changes) make up 60–70 per cent[8] of our communication. These speak as loudly – if not louder – than the words that we hear.

Conversation Rebels know that **building empathy** is the most powerful tool to create engagement.

I've heard empathy described as being like a muscle you can strengthen over time. But what exactly is empathy? And how does it relate to sympathy or compassion for that matter?

I visualise sympathy, compassion and empathy as a three-step ladder. The first step is sympathy, which is feeling bad for someone or taking pity on them. Compassion is the middle step, where you feel *with* someone who is suffering and where you might be able to impart some comfort. The third step is empathy. You've had to progress past sympathy and compassion to reach the empathy step. From the top deck you can see the entire landscape where you understand how someone feels emotionally and you view the world from their perspective.[9]

According to Dr Debra Keenahan, a psychologist and artist from Sydney, empathy is also a reflection of being comfortable with emotion; not just someone else's but also our own. It is central to helping us connect, build and collaborate.

And yet empathy appears to be in a state of decline at the moment. Research into the behaviour of American students found that empathy levels had almost halved from 1979–2009.[10] In the media you find frequent examples of people who don't behave with empathy or who lack good communications skills. But empathy can be taught. We can even teach ourselves and those around us to have more of it. And then it's our responsibility to practise what we've learned.

In her work, Dr Keenahan assumes the role of both subject and researcher. She's produced an immersive video entitled *Being Debra,* based on her personal experience with dwarfism. In the video, Debra shows how strangers react to her and her daughter, who also lives with dwarfism, while they are out and about.

At an exhibition called The Empathy Clinic, I donned a virtual reality headset to get a 3D experience of what it is like to be abused and cajoled by a group of strangers (played by actors) in a park. With the headset I gained Debra's perspective; I saw her legs under me, the faces of the abusers moving ominously towards me, all taunting smiles as if everyone except me is in on the joke. I sensed the aggression. I felt extremely vulnerable. What a relief to take the headset off. It was a courageous and creative piece of art.

Unfortunately, Debra told me she's belittled on a regular basis. 'All I want to do is walk down the street in peace but the abuse is always the same.' She continues:

> *The word 'dwarf' is never used as an insult. People use 'midget' which is an absolute insult. You feel it viscerally; it's the equivalent of an extreme racial slur. I always get abused in exactly the same way; they always use two words. The first starts with the letter 'F' and then 'midget'. And more often than not, they repeat it. And it's always yelled. And of course, it's always yelled from a distance. So, you wonder about the person saying it, 'Are you trying to draw attention to yourself?' Just what exactly is the dynamic going on here?'*

It was disheartening learning what Debra can experience once she leaves the safety of home. I felt sympathy for her (and anger). But after listening to her personal story and attending her exhibitions, I became emotionally and intellectually drawn to understand her encounters. Now I'm sharing that understanding and inviting you to reflect on it. That is what empathy does.

A simple starting point for harnessing empathy is to look closely at someone when you talk to them. When I started *One Plus One* in 2010, I developed a set of ground rules which gave the show its flavour and purpose. It was to be a show with an interviewer talking with a single guest. I never interviewed couples together. Using professional lighting, the camera crew created an intimate space wherever we recorded the interviews. The subject matter was broadly life, work and motivation. Sometimes I spent more time on a guest's career; sometimes the discussion was more about life (and death). However, the rule that stuck for nearly every one of the 500 conversations was that I looked directly at the guest. We locked eyes for thirty minutes.

'Making eye contact is among the very first human experiences,' says Dr Helen Riess, author of *The Empathy Effect*. 'When we speak to someone face to face, a process similar to those initial maternal gazes occurs, sending information about ourselves through another person's eyes.'[11]

When I look my conversation partner **directly in the eye,** it's as if we touch souls.

They have my full attention and the conversation proceeds like a duet. Neuroscientists, as it turns out, have shown that eye contact is one way to activate the regions in the brain involved with empathy.[12]

What if you find yourself speaking with someone who's vision-impaired? What do they do in the absence of eye contact? Former Disability Discrimination Commissioner Graeme Innes was born blind and was one of my interview guests some years ago. Graeme said that from a young age his mother prompted him to look at her when she spoke because that was expected behaviour from all of her children. Later as a lawyer, Graeme trained himself to constantly assess the body language of the people he's talking with. For example, were they sitting forward and listening attentively or was their voice further away and did they seem distracted? This skill is something he's worked on over the years. He even calls people out when he senses they aren't paying attention.

There are other examples I can think of when eye contact loses its importance. When I worked as a war correspondent in Iraq, many of the men I interviewed wouldn't look me in the eyes. Eye contact for any length of time is considered disrespectful in many cultures. There are also different habits related to gender, personal space and age, for instance, which can help or hinder an interaction or an outcome. This is where it pays to do a bit of research.

I'm often asked whether I have ever interviewed people I didn't like. Definitely there were a handful. And over the course of my career there were occasions when I interviewed people whose actions I didn't respect. My job wasn't to judge, but to listen to people and try to understand their motivation. Whether I liked them or not wasn't really relevant. I try to use the same frame when I meet and talk to people for the first time.

Sometimes, conversations just don't go according to plan, like the time I interviewed Lisa Genova. Lisa is the best-selling author of *Still Alice*, about an academic living with early-onset Alzheimer's disease.

With her make-up in place and looking amazing, Lisa slid elegantly into the TV studio. I expected her to be outgoing but to my surprise, she was quite reserved. The cameramen were in tweaking mode, trying to get their camera shots to match. This was my least favourite part of the taping because once I ran out of polite conversation, it was always tempting to use some of the questions I intended to ask during the interview, which I didn't do as a rule. I tried never to divulge my interview questions before the cameras started to roll. On this occasion, the cameramen continued to tweak and sitting in silence didn't feel right.

So, to fill the void I became chatty Jane.

I recall making a throwaway comment that Lisa looked 'big' in her publicity photo. What I *meant* to say was that she was smaller than I imagined, which is something people often say when they meet me (and others who appear on TV) in person. Out of the corner of my eye, I caught my producer shaking her head. Lisa appeared rattled by my comment. She turned to her publicist and queried which publicity photo I was referring to.

I began to get nervous, rapidly veering towards panicky. I tried to dig myself out of the hole I had made, realising I was doing the opposite of putting Lisa at ease. I said something along the lines of, while she was physically small, I'd imagined her as being larger than in her photo. That comment was greeted with silence. The explanation, not surprisingly, didn't have the intended calming effect.

By the time the recording started, Lisa had developed a scratchy throat. We stopped the interview a few times while she sipped water, but the coughing didn't completely stop. In fact, the tickle persisted through the interview. She only seemed completely relaxed when I said, 'Lisa, that's all we have time for, thanks so much for joining me.'

Thankfully – and it's why I love television – the magic of video-editing transformed the interview and removed Lisa's coughing. But the experience was an excellent demonstration of the power of misunderstanding. It's astonishing how quickly a few throwaway comments can get out of control. After all the research I'd done, I didn't manage to build empathy or connection. Instead of being the icebreaker, I was the icemaker, the irony being that Lisa's story was about her own search for empathy.

Lisa's grandmother had been diagnosed with Alzheimer's disease, a common type of dementia, when Lisa was nineteen. That experience made her want to understand what it was like to live with the condition. 'Fiction is the place where we can walk in someone else's shoes,' she said. Many years later, it was Lisa's turn to face one of life's great challenges.

'I was thirty-three, newly divorced and unemployed. Instead of doing the reasonable, responsible thing of going back to work where I would actually be paid and everybody around me would be okay, I decided instead *not* to do that. I would drop my daughter off at preschool and began writing a novel instead.'

That novel was *Still Alice*. After self-publishing and selling copies from the back of her car, a major publishing house eventually read the manuscript and agreed to publish it. Success didn't stop there. Lisa later sold the film rights resulting in *Still Alice* the movie, starring Julianne Moore.

I mentioned earlier that I didn't think of empathy as a muscle. I think of it as a daily practice like meditation or Pilates. I try to practice empathy with people who are outside my immediate circle, which feels good for me as an individual and beneficial for society. Empathy, according to author and scientist Dr Helen Riess, is what enables parents to see their children for who they are, helps businesses to thrive because they invest in their staff and allows politicians to represent the needs of their constituents.

What about people who commit heinous crimes? People like Ted Bundy or Ivan Milat, for instance – do they deserve our empathy? While we may not be able to find empathy for their actions, it's still possible to treat them with respect. It doesn't mean you understand their perspective or agree with what they've done but by treating them this way you condemn the behaviour rather than dehumanise the individual.[13]

In the meantime, harking back to my Lisa Genova story, I'd suggest you refrain from commenting on someone's physical appearance unless it's to say how fabulous they look.

Here are some other strategies to help you make connections using empathy.

Try It Out

Initiating conversation

I don't use the phrase 'small talk' as it implies parts of a discussion are insignificant. Having said that, some people find it challenging to initiate conversation. A little preparation helps. Think of putting yourself in someone else's shoes. If you ask something meaningful and specific you'll be on the way developing more empathy.

Introduce people with thoughtful detail

Consider the successful introduction from *Bridget Jones's Diary*. Even though Bridget has an alternative script playing in her head, she outwardly introduces her colleague, Perpetua, to her soon-to-be love interest, Mark Darcy: 'Ah, Perpetua. This is Mark Darcy. Mark's a top barrister. He comes from Grafton Underwood. (Turning to Mark) Perpetua's one of my work colleagues.'

If an introduction is succinct and relevant, it's easy to recall later. 'Oh yes, I met that woman who used to be an ABC foreign correspondent and is now writing about the art of conversation.'

Keep it brief and practise making a few introductions (or write them down) before the gathering.

On answering the question – 'What do *you* do?'

Nobody likes to be judged. Everyone likes to be respected. If I'm asked this, I try to be funny. 'Not much!' I might say. For some people, like stay-at-home mums or dads or if you're between jobs, it can be a challenging question because there's often a negative attitude to work that isn't paid. Try workshopping some responses so you're not caught short. Or try these:

> 'I manage an enterprise of four people (who all live under the same roof).'
>
> 'I've just learned to bake incredible sourdough bread.'
>
> 'I do exactly what I've always wanted to do.'
>
> 'I work for my family (and I bet my job is a lot harder than yours!).'
>
> 'I'm between jobs at the moment.'

Sometimes the asker or initiator could consider putting a bit more thought into an opening question. I like to listen to how people introduce themselves and then pick up a point of interest. For example, in a group I was travelling with recently, a man described himself as a beef farmer.

Here's how I carried the conversation forward:

Me: Has the farm been in your family for generations?

Him: No. I got fed up with the family farm so I sold it. But then I missed the life, so I bought a much smaller farm.

Me: I guess there's a big responsibility in keeping a large property …

Him: Yep. And I wanted to grow other produce on the farm. These days you have to diversify.

Be proactive

If a group conversation seems to be faltering, jump in and become a facilitator, encouraging everyone to share something about themselves.

'What's changed since I saw you at the park in September?'

'Have you finished that project on the cables yet? How did it finish up?'

'Do you think we will ever see our workplaces in the same way again?'

'I've put on six kilos! What are some of the new habits you've taken on?'

'Tell me, how did you learn to put a podcast together so quickly?'

A healthy habit

A colleague recently asked me what I'd been up to and I told her I'd been to see *Hamilton* the musical with my daughter. Without hesitation the colleague replied: 'I saw *Hamilton* on Broadway and then in London. In fact, me and my family were given free tickets.' This is known as one-upmanship, but I recently heard someone who does this described as a 'topper', which I rather liked. The topper thinks they're being enthusiastic, while they're really boasting or self-promoting. Often toppers don't realise what they are doing – and research backs this up. Toppers tend to overestimate how proud and happy a recipient feels for them and underestimate the other person's annoyance.[14]

If I find I've been topped by a topper, I might politely respond with a question about their Broadway experience and then I'll go back to what I was starting to say about the special evening with my daughter.

Do you suspect that you might be a topper? When someone tells you they held a koala for the first time on the weekend, do you respond by casually mentioning that you recently swam with whale sharks at Ningaloo Reef? Try to notice how the other person reacts. Do they seem a bit put out? If so, pause for a moment and consider that you've just knocked the stuffing out of them. You could even apologise.

A healthier approach for a would-be topper is to ask a follow-up question or two about my night out and then match my energy with yours so we can mutually bask in the excitement of *Hamilton* – whether viewed on Broadway, the West End, or in Sydney.

Perhaps you can articulate *what* was special about the performances? If both players finish the conversation feeling they've been listened to and appreciated in equal amounts, that's a much better outcome.

Maggie's rule

Margaret Court, Australia's most successful female tennis player turned Pentecostal pastor, describes herself as an 'anonymous champion'. She didn't much like the interview I did with her. Her disparaging comments about same-sex marriage and LGBTQIA+ people can make for robust conversation. She once told a newspaper that interviewers (including me) didn't seek to understand her point of view. 'It would have been nice if they had come from "Why do you have such strong beliefs in this area?"' she said. Margaret makes a valid point. I can't recall the last time I changed my view because someone berated me.

It doesn't mean, however, you shouldn't try to challenge people on their views. Refugee advocate and barrister Julian Burnside told me that some years ago, he started receiving hate mail as a result of his defence work. 'It's amazing how rude people are willing to be,' he said. 'They write to someone they've never met, swearing and cursing and abusing. It's extraordinary.'

Julian decided to write back to the critics giving them a few facts. He wrote 'Dear, so-and-so, thank you for your email, I gather you disagree with me, but did you realise ...?' He said, 'Almost all of them wrote back to me. And what struck me was that every answer was polite. They'd gone from screaming to polite in a single step.' What's more, he said, many of the critics conceded that they hadn't known all the facts.

Some even changed their minds.

Chapter Four

Be Curious

Years ago, I was offered an interview with ex-criminal, Mark Brandon Read, aka Chopper. If you search online, you'll see a man wearing a black leather jacket, covered in tattoos with chipped teeth and a ripped ear. His life-story reads like a blockbuster script and not surprisingly, he did indeed become the subject of a film starring actor and comedian Eric Bana.

From the ages of 20–38, Chopper was only out of prison for a year. Convicted of arson, assault, kidnapping and armed robbery, on his release he began to write for a living: several semi-autobiographical crime novels and, believe it or not, children's books.

At first, I agreed to interview him on my show. But then I worried how this might appear. This guy didn't look like most of the people I interviewed. He wasn't a hero. He had a few more tattoos than most. He was intimidating. What would people think? Would the publicity from our interview enable him to profit from his former life?

Eventually, I made the decision to pull out. It's a decision that has weighed on me to this day. Sometimes I think turning down the Chopper interview was one of the worst decisions I've ever made. Why? Because I threw away a potentially great conversation. You only have to look at Chopper's bio to see that.

His early years didn't have the nourishing foundation that many children get. He lived in an orphanage until the age of five. His mother, who held religion above everything else, told him that she didn't consider his birth a gift from God. His war-veteran father slept next to a gun. When the boy was eventually reunited with his parents, his father beat him. By the age of fifteen, Chopper had already been in several hundred fights. In his final TV interview, he claimed to have murdered four people, for which he was never charged.

A few years ago, crime-writer Adam Shand's biography of Chopper described him as 'a cartoon character created by Mark Brandon Read'. He continued, 'We wanted this anti-hero to be true. He gave some people hope, [to] others he [was] someone to judge and condemn. He was a tangle of contradictions.'[15] Three years after I was offered the interview, Chopper died of cancer. I didn't get to ask him about his tough-love upbringing or to understand his slide into criminality.

So far, I've discussed:

Readiness (Preparation) and

Empathy (Connecting).

Being curious is the third element of Rebel talk. 'The most important thing is not to stop questioning,' said Albert Einstein in an essay published in *Life Magazine* in 1955. 'Curiosity has its own reason for existence. One cannot help but be in awe when contemplating the mysteries of eternity, of life, of the marvellous structure of reality. It is enough if one tries merely to comprehend a little of this mystery each day.'[16]

I use curiosity as a frame to participate in conversations that I may not be looking forward to. I enjoy discovering new knowledge, understanding and experiences, so for me, setting an intention like: 'In this conversation I'm hoping to learn something new about …' helps to focus my motivation. For instance, maths is not one of my strong points. But I'm hopeful I'll eventually find inspiration in maths by keeping an open mind (being curious) and asking lots of questions. And while I may not pick up a book entitled *The Joy of Maths*, I'd happily read a biography of a mathematician or a scientist who changed the world through their brilliance and perseverance.

?

One of the most inquisitive people I've met is a ninety-two-year-old named Robin. His life has been filled with hobbies, service and learning. Robin has an excellent recall of his childhood in 1930s Shanghai including an incident when pirates captured him and his family as they travelled between cities. Pirates boarded the ship they were on and ordered the passengers to turn over all their valuables. Robin's mother lost her wedding ring and a much-loved portable gramophone player. Weeks later, what remained of the handsome gramophone was returned in tiny fragments. Happily, the family remained intact and spent five more years in China until Robin's father retired and the family emigrated to Sydney.

Robin didn't qualify for university. He became a journalist working on a manufacturing magazine and then for *The Sydney Morning Herald*, first in Sydney and then in London. He took a sub-editor position in Hong Kong, met his future wife (also a journalist) and after a long career in newspapers, was awarded a Commander of the British Empire (CBE) by the Queen.

The thing is, Robin never really retired. After journalism he wrote books about artists and several corporate histories. Work and discipline were always central to his philosophy. Retirement meant following his curiosity and he usually did that by reading. In his seventies and eighties to keep his memory sharp, he read up on a diverse range of topics from science to Middle-Eastern history and delivered weekly lectures at a community centre. At the age of 90, he was ordained as a lay deacon.

Robin continues to help people in need. He is carer to Beatrice, his 98-year-old wife – who has dementia – and, at the time of writing, they still lived at home. To this day, when I visit their apartment, there's a book open on the coffee table and he's ready with a documentary recommendation or a discussion about something that's captured his attention from the news.

I happen to know Robin because he's my dad. He doesn't think of himself as being particularly curious, but when my brothers and I were growing up, the shelves always bulged with books bought for enjoyment and learning. You might say Robin is a constant seeker. Learning is how he feels fully alive.

Remember Albert Einstein's quote from earlier in the chapter? 'The most important thing is not to stop questioning'. Well, the best way to be curious is to ask good questions.

Our early lives are filled with questions. Between the ages of two and five, a child asks around 40,000 explanatory questions. Younger children learn from their parents and carers that it's safe to ask. Then between the ages of five and eighteen something shifts, according to the research. Older children don't ask many questions. It's not because they become less curious, it's because adults stop listening or questions aren't encouraged.[17]

As an interviewer, I developed a question-making process which went like this:

- collect biographical information and issues I'm thinking of discussing
- read widely for different perspectives
- decide how to ask the questions.

I would ask myself: What do I want to achieve by asking a question a certain way? How do I build a guest's trust and confidence? What's a more interesting way to ask the question or to challenge or delight a guest?

While it was always fun interviewing celebrities, actors and comedians, some of my favourite interviews were with people who were not famous but who'd led fascinating lives. Sex-worker advocate Julie Bates AO was one of these.

In the week our interview was to be broadcast, she discovered a news outlet had described her as a *former* sex-worker. She sought a correction to acknowledge that she was very much a 'current' sex-worker and proud of it. Julie's work involved visiting aged-care facilities (at the request of residents or their families) to provide 'intimate services' to those deprived of human touch.

As we sat in the studio waiting for the TV director's signal to start the interview, I kept thinking about my intention; I wanted Julie to feel relaxed and I wanted to help her tell her story in a respectful and compassionate way. Our conversation challenged many of my negative assumptions about sex work, for instance, she freely chose the profession. For me, it's always the conversation that changes my views or beliefs that I find the most satisfying.

How do you ask questions that don't sound judgemental? Don't expect to already know the answer, and give your conversation partner the space and opportunity to respond. Here's what I mean:

One way (closed questions)	Another way (open-ended questions)
You worked in a law firm. Did that give you the idea that sex work could be a good career move?	Why did you become a sex worker?
Were you always well-treated by your clients?	How did your clients treat you?

Do you consider sex work a job like any other?

What do you say to those who insist sex work isn't a legitimate career?

Do you accept that in some parts of the world, women don't choose to be sex workers?

What is your take on how sex work is viewed in countries such as China?

Is there still shame and stigma attached to your profession?

What do you tell your grandchildren about what Granny does?

Are you proud of your Order of Australia award?

How are you going to make the most of your award?

I'm often asked: 'What constitutes a great question?'

Here's one I really like: Why are you at Harvard Law School, taking the place of a man?'

The Dean of Harvard Law School asked this of nine female students in 1956, six years after the school began admitting women. They were nine women out of a class of 500. One of them was the trailblazing Ruth Bader Ginsberg who went on to an extremely successful career, eventually becoming an associate justice of the United States Supreme Court before her death in September 2020.

Let's look closely at the question again: 'Why are you at Harvard Law School, taking the place of a man?'

Here are some possible reactions:

> How dare the dean ask that question!
>
> He was trying to get to know his new students.
>
> He was genuinely interested how they came to be in the class.
>
> He was deliberately courting controversy.
>
> He was out of line.

I like the question because:

> It's curious.
>
> It reveals the power to provoke.
>
> It's understated.
>
> It's simple.
>
> It's memorable.

Mostly, it's a great question because it causes you to lose your footing ever-so slightly. In the momentary pause after the question is asked, the respondent might exclaim, 'That's a great question,' before they attempt to answer it.

Here's another question I like for its simplicity: 'Why is the sky dark at night?' The answer eluded astronomers for 200 years.

A good question must pose a challenge and can often stay with you for days or even years.

Unfortunately, as creatures of habit, we humans can get lazy and persist with questions that don't go anywhere. Many parents, for instance, ask their kids rote or incurious questions. 'How was your day?' Probably doesn't produce an interesting response at the end of school when a child is tired. But if you remember what your child was supposed to be doing and get specific, 'How did your speech go, did the other kids enjoy it? Were you nervous?' the response might produce more detail and you can add some follow-up questions which aren't overly taxing:

> Really? And what else?
>
> Can you explain that?

In public life, in the media and online, questions have become a popular way to present information. Mostly though, these are not Rebel questions.

Here's a few I heard recently:

> What happens when we put poison on the ground near the lizards? (Zookeeper to school group)
>
> Why don't *we* have that type of mask? (Health administrator to staff)
>
> Wouldn't you agree? (Leading question from a journalist)
>
> Tell me a bit about yourself. (Job interview direction)

Questions can lead to discovery and understanding. But they can also be obstacles in our conversations when they are used to disempower:

> Do you understand what you got wrong?
>
> Shouldn't you have known better?

There are also the occasions when we are discouraged from asking the right questions because:

- we don't want to look stupid
- the environment is hostile or disapproving
- we're too busy to think of better questions
- we haven't been taught to ask good questions.

You can ask Google anything, even 'conversation starters to break the ice at dinner parties and events.' But Rebels know that the best questions are the ones we create ourselves. As former CNN interviewer and now Professor of Media and Public Affairs, Frank Sesno writes in his book *Ask More*, 'Sincere questions play second fiddle to certainty, ideology and outrage. But what if we asked more and asserted less? What would we discover? How much better would we understand the people around us? What if we went asking for solutions and posed truly creative questions that could change the world?'[18]

Try It Out

Instead of giving advice, ask questions

My daughter was keen to get her ears pierced. I wanted the technician to ensure she had the holes marked evenly, but I knew it would sound wrong if I told her, 'Make sure you get them even,' so I held my tongue. She made a dot on each ear. Then she rubbed them off and started again several times.

Now was my chance. 'How do you get the holes in exactly the right place?' I asked her.

'I have to be very precise,' she replied. 'I hate it when I get it wrong, so I have to be spot on.' When the technician felt she had the pen marks just right, she asked me what I thought. That was good collaboration. We were safe in her hands and the result was perfect.

In the workplace, academia, in government, good leaders should resist the urge to give advice all the time. Haven't we had enough already? By asking questions and gently challenging, leaders help their colleagues discover their own solutions.

Avoid hackneyed questions

> How's your day been so far?
>
> What are you getting up to for the rest of the day?
>
> Would you like to see some of our most popular styles?

Scripted questions are for robots and make many customers feel depersonalised. Try to read your customers' expressions and think of something specific to ask:

> Would you like to try some of the chocolate tart? Our chef is famous for it!
>
> Is there anything I can show you or are you happy to look around by yourself?
>
> It's been hot here today. Are you used to weather like this?

There's no such thing as a stupid question, but it may have been asked before (many times)

Prolific Scottish author Alexander McCall-Smith (*No. 1. Ladies Detective Agency* series and many others) says the question asked of authors at every literary festival is 'Where do you get your ideas from?'[19] While he acknowledges the question can be annoying (or a 'heartsink' question, as he nicely describes it) it's also valid: 'The real answer is *from out there*, which covers a multitude of possibilities – chance remarks, overheard conversations, newspaper reports, things said and unsaid, dreams.' I would add travel experiences, art, listening to interviews and Q&A sessions.

Public Q&A sessions can be wonderfully inspiring. They can also be dominated by punters making long statements or asking rambling questions. Don't be afraid to put your hand up to ask. At the same time, think of the community around you and work up the best, most succinct, creative question you can in the time available.

Make a note of good questions you hear around you. If you feel you haven't quite captured the essence of a question you're formulating, try letting it marinate for a few hours or even a few days. Read your questions out aloud and sharpen them up; fix the grammar, lose unnecessary words, remove inconsistencies, clarify the meaning. Think of the questions that precede and follow and how the list works together.

Creating questions is good for your brain. The brain gets active as it reflects, releasing the hormone serotonin which promotes relaxation and relieves stress. This encourages intelligence gathering from all areas of the brain allowing more insight than if you were merely delivering solutions to others.[20]

Once you've mastered the art of asking questions, a conversation Rebel needs to be all ears for the next skill.

Chapter Five

Engage Attention: the art of humble listening

'Everything is a stepping-stone to something else,' says actor Alan Alda, a man who's taught himself how to listen. 'I'm always looking to get better. It will never be perfect.'[21]

Alda, now in his mid-eighties, is the much-loved star of the 1970s hit TV series *M*A*S*H*. He owes his heightened sense of awareness to an unusual childhood; his father was an actor, singer and dancer on Broadway. His mother, a former beauty queen, lived with mental health issues. Alan himself didn't escape a life of challenge either; as a child, he contracted polio.

'It was what life was,' he said of his childhood.

> *One of the most valuable experiences for me growing up was spending hours and hours daydreaming, lying on my back, looking at the clouds, trying to figure things out or letting fantasies build in my head. Our living room was lined with books chosen by an interior decorator for their leather bindings … stuff I didn't understand but could imagine. These were formative experiences that led in some way to what I do now.*

Despite a diagnosis of Parkinson's disease in 2015, in recent years Alan has championed the importance of communication and specifically communicating science.[22]

He was offered a role hosting a science show on TV which he did for eleven years after a long acting career. For the series he interviewed hundreds of experts about their breakthroughs in science, engineering and medicine.

Alda realised that there was a shortcoming in how scientists communicated. When they talk to the public about their work, he found, they talk about the end result before the discovery.

> *It's a story told backwards. They don't tell you what the obstacles were, the disasters that occurred, the wrong turns they took in getting to their final discovery. That's*

> *where the drama is. That's where we realize that science is a human experience. These people aren't gods. They're not secret masters of the universe. They have the same way of working things out that we do.*

Working with these scientists encouraged him to establish the Alan Alda Center for Communicating Science. And here's where I was hooked; after a lifetime of talking, Alda declared that he was ready to listen, 'I have this radical idea that I'm not really listening unless I'm willing to be changed by you.'[23]

I've borrowed Alda's radical idea on listening and change. Research suggests that while we spend 45 per cent of communication time listening, we are poor and inefficient listeners.[24] This made me wonder, how can we be good at conversation if we're bad at listening?

I thought this might be a good place for some self-reflection, which in my view is a highly recommended trait for a Rebel.

So here's a self-assessment exercise.

The Rebel Conversation self-audit

Answer honestly — yes, no or maybe — and feel free to write the answers on the page. You can also download the questions as a PDF at my website: www.janehutcheon.com

1. I tend to talk over the top of other people
2. I feel comfortable talking with anyone I meet
3. My partner/close friend/parent tells me I lecture her/him
4. I feel fearful and/or anxious when talking with someone for the first time
5. I am a confident, fluent conversationalist
6. I stumble and/or mumble when I'm having a conversation
7. I am confident at initiating conversations
8. I make eye contact when speaking with someone
9. I tap my foot, fiddle with jewellery or hair when I speak with someone
10. I don't remember my conversations because they're not that interesting
11. I'm an excellent listener
12. I'm comfortable being in an argument

13. I avoid conflict at all cost
14. Other people feel uncomfortable around me but I'm not sure why
15. I've heard myself described as a know-all
16. I've never thought about the power of questions before
17. At meetings/conferences I linger in the middle of the room and say very little except to people I know
18. Conversation isn't a difficult skill. You just open your mouth and speak
19. I know several people at work who qualify as 'loudmouths' but I am definitely not one of them
20. I often pick-up shortcomings in other peoples' conversation skills
21. People often ask me for my opinions
22. I enjoy giving people advice because it helps them

Did the self-audit shine a light on some things you were aware of subconsciously?

Let me tell you about a time I learned something important about listening.

Years ago, I made a TV documentary about China's bid to host the 2000 Olympic Games. I travelled to Beijing one blistering summer to interview a top official in charge of the bid. The crew and I sat in bumper-to-bumper traffic with the cars around us using horns like they were having animated conversations: I'm merging now! Here I come! Don't you see me? Look out!

By the time we arrived and stepped into the cool, marble-floored office, a man dressed like a factory foreman jumped up to shake my hand. It turned out he was the official I was about to interview.

The lights and cameras went up. The interview began and I settled in for a long session with the interpreter, who was a friend of mine, sitting by my side. During the interview, the official became agitated when we discussed the subject of human rights. I asked about America pressuring China over its treatment of dissidents. His response went on for several minutes. The room got very warm since the camera crew had turned off the air-conditioner and I began to feel drowsy. Interpreted interviews always require a bit more of your attention while you wait for the translation.

The official started talking about the upcoming Olympic Games in Atlanta and I perked up. When the translator shared what had been said, it was along the lines of 'China should boycott the upcoming US games in retaliation for America's criticism of China's human rights record.'

Hello, I thought. Did I hear that correctly?

I checked with the translator, mirroring the words back to her, 'China should boycott the upcoming US games in Atlanta?'

'That's right.' she said. I asked the question again – twice – to make sure I correctly heard the answer. Two more times, the translator repeated the assertion:

'China should consider boycotting the Atlanta Olympic Games in retaliation for American criticism of human rights in China.'

Were the official's comments a big deal? Did I have a scoop?

Returning to Sydney a few weeks later, I mentioned the interview with the official to my colleagues. They didn't react. It didn't *seem* Earth-shattering. I shrugged it off and wrote the documentary script. The program was scheduled for broadcast right before the final vote on which city was going to host the 2000 Olympics. Days before the broadcast, I mentioned the exchange with the official again, this time to the show's publicity manager.

'That sounds amazing!' she said.

'But the rest of the team doesn't think so,' I told her.

'Well, I'm going to make that part the lead paragraph in my press release.'

And she did.

In those pre-internet days, after the press release was sent out, it didn't take long for the phones to start ringing. Reuters, Associated Press, the BBC. Within a few hours, our newsroom was converted into a call centre. Leading international news organisations interviewed me and ran excerpts from my documentary. Finally, in the vote for the host city, Sydney, and not Beijing, won the right to host the 2000 Olympic Games – by a slim two votes.

There haven't been many scoops in my career. But I got lucky on this occasion *and* I'd been paying attention. It would have been easy to gloss over what the official said or to tune-out because I felt drowsy. As Rebels, when we train ourselves to tune-in to significant conversations it can really pay off. But there's another type of listening I want to share with you that goes even further in terms of connecting and validating the person you are listening to.

Robert Manne is an Emeritus Professor of Politics at La Trobe University, a public intellectual and author. He was a regular guest on TV panel shows. Rob Manne's ideas were his calling card. Then he disappeared from public life. A few years later a book of his essays called *On Borrowed Time* appeared. I was offered an interview with him but couldn't decide if I should go ahead. You see, Rob had recently undergone surgery for throat cancer. His larynx (or voice box) had to be removed and his throat reconstructed. After a brief phone discussion and with some hesitation on my part, I agreed to go ahead.

As Rob made himself comfortable in the TV studio, I noticed he was wearing a polo-neck skivvy under his shirt to cover where the surgery had been. He asked for the microphone to be placed as near as possible to his throat, rather than close to his mouth. As always, I began by welcoming my guest and explaining to viewers that we were going to hear Rob as we'd never heard him before. He began to speak, using his right hand to depress his stoma (opening in the throat). That redirects the airflow so, in the absence of a voice box, the tongue and teeth do the work of speaking.

Rob's new voice emerged as a whisper. As he said, speaking that way felt like he was telling you his deepest secrets. Decades ago, one of my dad's friends underwent a similar operation. Though this man loved to talk, I never understood more than 30 per cent of what he was saying and I was afraid to admit it to him. With Rob, initially I panicked. The voice in my head said 'I can't hear him!', but by blocking out distractions, I focused on the voice and the expression on Rob's face. He was telling me a story about a radio producer who said his new voice would be 'unendurable'.

Rob is an eloquent storyteller. I learned that as a boy, he cared for his dying mother and had found hospitals distressing since that time. But during his cancer treatment he experienced a transformation, seeing hospitals as 'cathedrals to the humanist spirit. Everything in its place, everything working.'[25]

Rob and I made it through the thirty-minute interview without any issues. I realised that my initial hesitation about interviewing him had nothing to do with his voice. The problem was to do with me. I lacked the patience to listen. Patience is only the first step in giving your full attention to someone and 'attention is the rarest and purest form of generosity,' according to philosopher Simone Weil.

'Attention is the rarest and purest form of generosity.'

Try It Out

Humble listening

Radio and TV presenter Yumi Stynes knows a thing or two about hate campaigns and social-media storms after an on-air clash with fellow commentator Kerri-Anne Kennerley.

Yumi used the phrase 'humble listening' when we discussed the row. To listen humbly is to respond without judgement and to remind yourself that you could be wrong. Yumi also suggests 'seeking out the voices of people who are downtrodden or less advantaged and then humbly listening to them. From that, you'll learn so much.'

Here's my take on humble listening:

- Imagine you and your conversation partner are in a cocoon.
- Remove distractions and put the smartphones out of sight.
- Look at the other person. Show them you are interested in the conversation. (When speaking to people with a disability try asking someone *how* they communicate and what you can do to support them.)
- Use curiosity (see *Chapter Four*) and ask questions.
- Don't force your ideas onto your conversation partner. Don't talk over them or interrupt them.

- Observe *how* they appear. What does their body language tell you? Do their words match their body language?
- When your conversation partner has finished speaking, try prompting them with questions to consolidate your understanding:
    - Is there anything else?
    - How did that feel?
    - How did you put that into perspective?
    - What do you believe now?
- Summarise out loud the main points your partner has shared with you. Ask whether you've understood them correctly.

Often when I interview people about personal matters; what parents meant to them, how they felt about being kicked out of home, the terrible accident that changed their lives, I notice their eyes tearing up. At that point I might say:

- How are you going there?
- This must be hard for you.
- Would you like to take a minute?
- Shall we stop the interview?
- What shall we talk about now?

It's fairly easy for me to *write* 'you need to listen intently'. And poor listening is clearly something corporations, communities and individuals have issues with because there are dozens of listening theories and scores of books on the subject (I like *Are You Listening* by Ralph G. Nichols and Leonard Stevens, written in the late 1950s). There's even an International Day of Listening every September! But honestly, listening is not rocket science. It is, however, a skill that can be improved.

WAIT

In broadcasting, silence in a conversation usually means there's a glitch or problem – we usually don't leave too much room for responses. So while interviewing someone who's softly spoken, like veteran performer Marcia Hines, I found myself asking many more questions than I normally do just to fill the pauses. By the time the half-hour was finished, I felt exhausted. In hindsight, I realised that I'd turned into a gasbag to compensate for Marcia's shyness. Now, whenever I feel the 'gasbag' approaching, I encourage myself to WAIT: Why Am I Talking?

WAIT: Why Am I Talking?

Though he didn't invent the acronym, actor Tom Hanks uses it as a reminder that listening is a discipline: 'I have to force myself to listen because I love the sound of my own voice and because I'm a movie star I've been infantilized by everybody I come across who says I'm just wonderful. "Look at you! You can stand up so good and you can eat with a fork! What a special, special, special movie star you are!"'[26]

Chapter Six

Lead the Way

A few years ago, my manager received an email from a viewer who wanted me fired.

The viewer (I'll call her Betty), said I'd committed several transgressions, the main one being that I insulted a former justice of the High Court of Australia, the Hon Michael Kirby AC CMG. In an interview, I asked him whether lawyers have too much power in society. Michael clearly didn't like the question. He defended the legal profession, naturally. Several viewers who saw the exchange congratulated me. But Betty said I'd been rude and disrespectful. To my knowledge, it was the first time a viewer had called for my dismissal. She used the word 'insolence' which sounded like a comment straight out of *Downton Abbey*.

Betty's reaction intrigued me. I wanted to get in touch with her to find out why she was offended, but I felt it was best left to my manager. I confess that it still plays on my mind; an unresolved conversation. But it made me think about how much our upbringing shapes both the way we converse and how we judge others.

So far, we've covered:

Readiness – research and preparation

Empathy – for connection

Be curious – asking questions

Engage attention – humble listening

Now we've reached the final tool in the acronym: **Lead the Way** – choosing how to respond.

While I grew up in a loving, supportive family, I was also taught to respect my elders and not to be overly talkative or argumentative. As a teenager I recall an argument with my mum when I decided to stand my ground. She reacted by shutting down the conversation. It became a waiting game. She refused to talk to me until I apologised. It was three days before I gave in. I don't even remember what the argument was about, but I remember feeling powerless at the time.

What I didn't understand was that my mum was brought up in an era when children were 'seen and not heard'. They didn't get to speak up for themselves or disagree with decisions that were made on their behalf. Parenting today, generally speaking, is more collaborative and respectful of a child's emotions.

I grew up wanting to please people around me. But after choosing my career, journalism helped me discover and explore my own voice, sometimes at the expense of upsetting people. Despite my best efforts, as a fallible human I'm still making mistakes in my conversations and despite every effort to improve, they are never going to be perfect. That doesn't stop me from trying.

So that's my conversation backstory in a nutshell. Perhaps this is a good moment for you to reflect on your backstory and what might be holding you back.

Earlier, I recounted the story about my throwaway comments to best-selling author Lisa Genova. There are other occasions when conversations don't go the way you expect them to and a friendship, personal or professional relationship comes unstuck.

According to experts at The Harvard Negotiation Project, difficult conversations (defined as conversations likely to involve conflict and/or which bring out a strong emotional response) are actually three separate conversations:

- *What happened* – fixation on truth, intentions and blame
- *The feeling conversation* – the role of emotions in our disputes
- *The identity conversation* – what the dispute says about how we see ourselves.

I discovered another conversation too: the one that plays out in your head.

Conversation type	Description
Conversation 1 (what happened)	My version versus your version.
Conversation 2 (emotional)	Both parties are upset but fail to articulate this.

Conversation 3 (identity)	What do your words and behaviour say about how I see myself?
Conversation 4 (internal)	Why can't you read my mind?

After a conversation goes wrong (or email exchanges are misunderstood or misread), it's useful to arrange a review between the parties, to talk about why the conversation faltered. This may not produce complete agreement, but can hopefully lead to a friendly truce or better still, greater understanding.

Of course, we don't always know what goes on in someone else's head. I was reminded of this just recently when a collaborator and I parted ways over a project in which they were acting as my representative. The collaborator did not respond eagerly to an offer to discuss what had scuppered the negotiation. Sometimes awkward outcomes can't be neatly packaged up and finished with silk ribbon.

There are plenty of occasions where an apology is in order. Many of us, including me, could strengthen our apology muscle. The apology muscle is attached to the courage muscle. Sometimes it takes time and contemplation to accept that you were wrong or that you've caused hurt and an apology should be offered. It takes work to train the muscle.

In an apology, simple is best.

Here are some examples of apologies:

I'm sorry I made a hurtful comment about your fiancée, but I was just trying to warn you.

No. There's no 'but' in an apology.

I'm sorry I made a hurtful comment about your fiancée. Can we be friends again?

Not quite. This lacks humility and remorse.

I'm sorry I made a hurtful comment about your fiancée. What was I thinking? I was an idiot! I know you love this woman very much. I want to apologise to her too. Can you ever forgive me?

Good one. Humble, remorseful, unequivocal. It shows you've listened and heard the other person. Now, let's hope the apology is accepted with equal generosity.

There is another category of difficult conversation where we expect to disagree with the person we're talking to.

I'm talking about tackling people over their religious beliefs, vaccine hesitancy, conspiracy theories and climate change to name just a few conversation topics.

When I look back at my interviewing career, I regret that I didn't interview more people I disagreed with. It's so much easier to connect with someone you admire and with whom you have something in common. We live in a world where 'cancel culture' trumps civilised debate, or as *The New York Times* explains, we end up with an 'emerging class of people – journalists, academics, opinion writers (who are) cancelled for bad, conservative or offensive opinions.'[27]

Even well-meaning people contribute to cancel culture without realising it. We often hear about the growing epidemic of food allergies but we don't talk enough about human intolerance. It's not your job to be the convincer-in-chief or the adviser-in-chief. Be the collaborator-in-chief or the WAITer-in-chief (See Chapter Five: Why Am I Talking). Remember Maggie's Rule from Chapter Three? Research shows people don't change their minds by being harangued or humiliated.[28]

In fact, trying to force your views on someone usually sends them in the opposite direction. If you want to change someone's mind, consider borrowing from a process called Motivational Interviewing, a counselling method which helps individuals explore and resolve hesitancy to change using the principle of RULE:

Resist the reflex to be right

Understand the person's motivations

Listen with empathy

Empower the individual

Motivational Interviewing evolved from the patient-centred counselling style of twentieth-century psychologist Carl Rogers who noted, 'The curious paradox is that when I accept myself just as I am, then I can change.'[29]

Do you remember in Chapter One when I spoke about being invited by my boss to an awards evening at an art gallery? I spoke of how the event made me feel so anxious I nearly turned around and left. Now I'm going to finish the story.

That night, something surprising happened. By the time the final winner was announced I realised that despite my apprehension, I was actually enjoying myself. I sat next to a lovely executive who told me she was newly hired and commuted by plane at the start of each week. I was able to introduce her to the city I love and gave her suggestions for places to stay.

Apart from the executive, I reconnected with a few people I hadn't seen in years, including the publicist who wrote the press release about my Olympics scoop. In turn, she gave me ideas from the list of award winners for future interviewees for my show. Apart from supporting my boss, once I found my feet I felt happy and connected. I was glad I hadn't missed out.

When we isolate ourselves, or we become isolated due to external reasons, we run against human nature according to Nicholas Epley, Professor of Behavioural Science at the University of Chicago, Booth School of Business. Despite this, we constantly underestimate the positive effect of being 'prosocial' (behaving in a way that benefits others or society as a whole including sharing, helping, donating, collaborating and volunteering). It turns out that connecting with another person, even on a commute with a stranger, has a positive impact on both people.

The last thing I want to share is that the saying 'time heals all wounds' isn't strictly correct. Most conversation wounds don't heal with time. They just fester. It's best to be direct and to move beyond the discomfort. Another way to look at it is to reframe the conversation. Instead of thinking of it as a difficult conversation, imagine it as a helping conversation. Find good things to say about the incident or person. Let them down gently but firmly.

And if you are the one on the receiving end of the helping conversation, summarise what you're being told and don't be afraid to ask questions if you don't understand why.

Try It Out

Take charge

A few years ago, I was trying to decide whether to leave my job and I made a list of pros and cons. The two sides of the list had a similar number of points and I just couldn't make a choice. There were positives and negatives. What was I supposed to do, flip a coin?

I can't remember exactly how I found philosopher Ruth Chang's Ted Talk – with over eight million views – 'How to make Hard Choices'. I may have even googled 'how to choose when everything is equal'. Ruth said:

> *When we choose between options that are on a par, we make ourselves the authors of our own lives. Instead of being led by the nose by what we imagine to be facts of the world, we should instead recognize that sometimes the world is silent about what we should do. In those cases, we can create value for ourselves by committing to an option. By doing so, we not only create value for ourselves but we also (re)create ourselves.*[30]

Committing to an option, making ourselves the authors of our own lives, re-creating ourselves. This is what I call leading the way and it's an essential part of being a Rebel. Ruth continues:

> *'When we choose between options that are on a par, we can do something really rather remarkable. We can put our very selves behind an option. Here's where I stand. Here's who I am.'*

How will *you* lead the way? How will you make hard choices? How will you take responsibility for your conversations, how will you show up, how will you create change?

Asking permission

I once upset a minor celebrity by raising, in an interview, something he'd done several decades earlier that he wasn't proud of.

Later, his publicist contacted me to discuss the matter. I had found out about the controversy from a reputable news website. And though I felt justified in asking the question, I realised after that experience that I should have asked permission before the interview. It's kinder than landing a hard question out of the blue. As well as asking permission, it's helpful to add the context in which you're asking.

Here are some examples:

- 'I hear that your mum has been battling Parkinson's disease. I want to ask because I know you do a lot of charity work in that area. Is that something we can talk about?'

- 'Is it correct that your dad had a drinking problem? Can I ask you about your own struggle with alcoholism?'
- 'Can we talk about your three marriages? I'm keen to know how you managed to bring up thirteen children.'

Packaging the message

Sometimes it's not just the tone that needs thought. It's about the dynamic, the character of the person you are delivering the message to and the words themselves. Is there a way of constructing the message so that it's more accessible for the person you are speaking with?

Instead of:	How about:
You're not listening to me!	Could I explain that issue to you again?
Pick up the mess in your room!	Could you put your worn clothes in the laundry basket?
Don't tell me to wear a mask!	Why is it necessary to wear a mask here when elsewhere it's not required?
Shut up!	I am trying to remember something. Could you give me a minute?

Know when to end

A recent Harvard study found that 98 per cent of conversations don't end when people want them to; they either finish too quickly, or they go on too long. This is because conversation partners have to navigate scores of hints and cues and usually hide their true desires from the other. While it's not polite to say, 'I'm done now,' I used to give a verbal signal to my interview guests which was, 'Before I let you go ...' Another nice way to bring a conversation to a close is to make a brief summary: 'Well, it's been lovely catching up with you and hearing about all your news.'

My thinking is, unless you're familiar with the person you are talking with; it's respectful to end a conversation sooner rather than later.

How to have a difficult conversation

Every tough conversation is individual and different, and no tool or template can cover every situation.

Some of the most difficult conversations I've been privy to have taken place in hospital emergency departments. When you are emotional and running on adrenaline, how can you be sure that you've understood what you've heard? How was the news delivered? How did you respond? Were further conversations necessary? Each of us will have many difficult conversations over the course of our lives whether breaking up with a partner, receiving bad news, explaining controversial decisions, starting a war or declaring peace.

As you know, I love acronyms. I find they're a useful tool for remembering big ideas. Here's a tool for a difficult conversation using 4W's and 'MACE':

Components	Actions and preparation
***W**hen*	Timing: will the other person be in the right frame of mind for the conversation?
***W**here*	Is the environment appropriate for the conversation?
***W**hat*	What traits or skills are called for: kindness, assertiveness, clarity, comfort?
***W**ho*	Who is receiving the message and what will assist them in understanding?
***M**essage*	Message(s) – is it/are they delivered clearly and concisely?
***A**cknowledgement*	Has the message been clearly received? Can you confirm this?
***C**larify*	What questions might the other person ask?
***E**nd*	What's the expected outcome and how will you achieve this?

Chapter Seven

The art of being human

Now that I've shared my Rebel approach to rethinking conversation with you, I have a confession. I realise that while I've done a great number of interviews, an interview is not a spontaneous conversation. It's a trimmed lawn with topiaries and fountains; it doesn't happen on its own.

I'm convinced, however, that interviewing skills can guide you, as they've guided me, to have richer conversations and greater self-awareness and confidence. If you enjoy listening and watching interviews in any form, this is an excellent resource in the art of being human.

I know this because viewers have told me so. When I presented my interview show, every week I received emails, private messages, posts and letters telling me how valuable it was *listening* to people talk about their life experience. When we feel part of the same community, our burdens are shared. Humanity lights up like a string of lanterns.

Some years ago, I interviewed *Wild* author Cheryl Strayed. We spent much of the conversation talking about the subject that has dominated her adult life: learning to live without her mother. A few days after Cheryl's interview was broadcast, I received this note from a viewer named Peter:

> *My beautiful wife, Glenys, died of ovarian cancer three and a half years ago, just weeks before she would have turned sixty-three. Just like Cheryl was with her mother immediately before she died, I was with Glenys. And just like Cheryl, I too read to my beloved in the last few hours of her life. I slept on a mattress on the floor for two or three months before she died. I wanted desperately to hold her in her last moments. But, alas, I didn't. I knew that Glenys's death was not far away. It was easy to tell. But I just could not stay awake any longer. I let go of Glenys's hand, rolled over, and fell fast asleep.*
>
> *Sometime later at about 5.30 am, my sister woke me and told me that Glenys had died. After I had kissed my wife and held her for the final time, I was completely and totally consumed with the whitest of white rage.*

I was ready to lash out, to explode, to destroy everything in my sight. I gathered myself and went for a walk around the gardens where I had walked with Glenys in the weeks before her death, until a calmness and peacefulness returned.

In grieving my loss, I developed some problems, the most significant of which was insomnia. After counselling, I discovered that without my beautiful wife and friend, I no longer enjoyed going to bed; I had not permitted myself to go to sleep.

After listening to Cheryl and hearing that she too had difficulty in accepting that she did not hold her mother as she died, I immediately viewed my situation from a different perspective: maybe, the reason for the insomnia was misplaced guilt; I should not have allowed myself to fall asleep and abandon Glenys at the moment of her death.

I felt an immediate sense of relief and warmth after listening to Cheryl's story. She was doing what any decent person would have done in the same circumstances. I had also been made aware that the dying sometimes choose their time to go, often to protect their loved ones.

For the first time in a few years, I will look forward to going to sleep.

Peter's story is a homage to the value and gift of humble listening. I'm indebted to him and the many people who've written to me and supported my work over the years. I never expected that an interview could benefit so many people.

Surveying the landscape of a world wearied by the pandemic, we are in a very different headspace compared with life before COVID-19. Many of us feel numb or burned out, the future uncertain.

Well, friends, there is no time to languish.

I've dedicated my life to rethinking conversation and honing listening skills, and that's where I need your help. What gives me optimism is that I've witnessed how humans come together to tackle pressing issues. If the anthropause, the shift in human behaviour during the pandemic I first mentioned in the introduction, has caused many of us to reappraise what's valuable and important, then change is possible. After pressing 'pause', we don't have to hit 'play' and return to how things were.

A quarter of a century ago, beloved theoretical physicist Stephen Hawking observed:

> *For millions of years, mankind lived just like the animals. Then something happened which unleashed the power of our imagination. We learned to talk and we learned to listen. Speech has allowed the communication of ideas, enabling human beings to work together to build the impossible. Mankind's greatest achievements have come about by talking, and its greatest failures by*

not talking. It doesn't have to be like this … All we need to do is make sure we keep talking.[31]

If we're to raise the bar and aspire to Rebel Talk, we need to challenge ourselves with one more question: How can we change the outcome?

Friends,
Rebels,
thank you
for listening.

Resources

Please check my website for the latest resources and information about workshops for your organisation or community: www.janehutcheon.com

If I Understood You, Would I Have This Look On My Face? Alan Alda, Random House 2018

Ask More Frank Sesno, AMACOM 2017

I'm Right and You're an Idiot James Hoggan, Grania Litwin New Society Publishers 2016

Conversation: How Talk Can Change Our Lives Theodore Zeldin, HiddenSpring 2000

The Empathy Effect Helen Riess, MD with Liz Neporent, Sounds True 2018

We Need to Talk Celeste Headlee

Curious – Ian Lesley, Quercus 2015

The Art of Gathering Priya Parker, Penguin Books 2018

The Fine Art of Small Talk Debra Fine, Piatkus 2005

Think Again Adam Grant, Ebury Publishing 2021

Ruth Chang Ted Talk: How To Make Hard Choices: www.ted.com/talks/ruth_chang_how_to_make_hard_choices

Big Brains Podcast: https://news.uchicago.edu/podcasts/big-brains/why-talking-strangers-will-make-you-happier-nicholas-epley

Gratitude

'To write a new book,' author Glennon Doyle told the *New Yorker*, 'I always feel like I have to become a new person.' I concur. During this metamorphosis, it turns out you also need the help, love and encouragement of a community of generous people.

In the early days of this project, Matthew McCarthy urged me on supported by the talented team at Clear Design (Laura Vigilante and Dayna Stiles) who developed my brand and website, cleverly built by efront. Matthew also read the manuscript and provided feedback. Claire Scobie and Bernadette Foley provided early encouragement. Thanks also to Penny Modra at *The Good Copy* for her enthusiasm and advice. Penny recommended editor Emily Weekes whose insight and clarity working on my first major draft was a game changer for me.

I was fortunate to have the advice of former Disability Discrimination Commissioner Graeme Innes and

ABC Disability Correspondent Nas Campanella who contributed to my understanding of eye-contact from the perspective of disability culture.

Thanks to ABC News for permission to use the transcripts of the 500-plus interviews I conducted for *One Plus One* from 2010-2019.

Special thanks to my dear manuscript advisers, Jennifer Wong, Suzanne Panagiotopoulos and Helen Hughes. You were tough *and* kind; the best of combinations. Thank-you for your commitment and friendship, which I treasure.

My dad Robin, also read the manuscript and provided feedback. Thanks also to Manuel Panagiotopoulos and Jen Wong for helping me understand the concept of 'yutori'.

A chance conversation with Michelle Newton, Marketing Director at Fiftyfive5.com, resulted in a major change to my beloved acronym. When I did this, everything I was trying to achieve fell into place.

I'm indebted to psychologist (artist, performer, friend and writer) Dr Debra Keenahan for embracing this project thoroughly. We discussed chapters during face-to-face conversations over coffee and lunch. Debra never 'corrected' my ideas. Instead, she challenged me to clarify my thinking and ultimately made my work so much stronger.

Sincere thanks to Jon MacDonald who is an excellent lunch companion and the best kind of publisher: a humble adviser and a big-picture thinker – something every author needs. Editor Alice Grundy deftly and kindly knocked my words into place and turned the manuscript into a book.

To Michael and Isla, thank-you always for your love and patience. On the occasions where the cloud of 'numbness' hung overhead, Michael encouraged me by telling me to run my own race and to 'be more you'. Isla is skilled at providing first-aid in its many forms.

Finally, to my darling mum Bea, who teaches me every day not to give up and that that love is always the final word.

Endnotes

1 https://www.scimex.org/newsfeed/the-anthropause-the-sound-of-seismic-silence-during-lockdown

2 Kind permission of www.Fiftyfive5.com: Covid Consumer Impact Monitor (March-September 2020)

3 Theodore Zeldin interview on 2010 Courage Beer survey: https://www.youtube.com/watch?v=5_r9Quv4o5Q

4 Kind permission of www.Fiftyfive5.com: Covid Consumer Impact Monitor (March-September 2020)

5 Professor Jerry Egan speaking on The Talking Revolution podcast: https://thetalkingrevolution.org/helping-understanding-and-revolution-a-conversation-with-gerard-egan/

6 https://www.theguardian.com/commentisfree/2017/sep/22/listen-up-australians-its-time-to-turn-down-the-volume

7 https://www.queensu.ca/gazette/stories/discovery-thought-worms-opens-window-mind

8 https://www.pgi.com/blog/2020/03/how-much-of-communication-is-really-nonverbal/

9 See Helen Riess, MD with Liz Neporent, The Empathy Effect

10 https://www.zurich.com/en/knowledge/topics/global-risks/decline-human-empathy-creates-global-risks-age-of-anger

11 Helen Riess, MD with Liz Neporent, The Empathy Effect p. 43

12 Helen Riess, MD with Liz Neporent, The Empathy Effect p. 46

13 https://www.police1.com/health-fitness/articles/why-respecting-even-the-most-vile-criminals-is-important-to-our-survival-Vpee2tQJoTuOlVqv/

14 https://www.researchgate.net/publication/276065186_You_Call_It_Self-Exuberance_I_Call_It_Bragging_Miscalibrated_Predictions_of_Emotional_Responses_to_Self-Promotion

15 https://www.smh.com.au/entertainment/question-time-adam-shand-on-the-real-chopper-20140916-10h1c4.html

16 'Old Man's Advice to Youth: 'Never Lose a Holy Curiosity.' *LIFE Magazine*, 2 May 1955 p. 64 Albert Einstein. I've edited the phrase to make it sound more modern.

17 https://www.greatschools.org/gk/articles/cracking-the-code-on-curiosity/

18 Frank Sesno Ask More – Page 2 Amacon, New York 2017

19 https://inews.co.uk/opinion/literary-festivals-ask-authors-ideas-edinburgh-hay-615462

20 https://www.govexec.com/management/2017/04/neuroscience-asking-insightful-questions/137274/

21 https://hbr.org/2017/07/alan-alda

22 (https://hbr.org/2017/07/alan-alda)

23 https://www.washingtonpost.com/lifestyle/2020/03/12/alan-alda-would-like-your-attention/?arc404=true

24 https://extension2.missouri.edu/cm150

25 https://www.theguardian.com/books/2017/aug/12/robert-manne-on-having-cancer-i-am-interested-in-why-i-felt-no-fear

26 https://www.postregister.com/features/ticket/tom-hanks-didn-t-want-to-be-mr-rogers-then/article_9cd-d440c-234e-56e6-9af7-05b1d56b337e.html

27 https://www.nytimes.com/2019/11/02/style/what-is-cancel-culture.html

28 https://www.psychologytoday.com/us/blog/think-well/201812/why-many-people-stubbornly-refuse-change-their-minds

29 https://positivepsychology.com/motivational-interviewing/

30 https://www.nytimes.com/2015/01/04/opinion/sunday/resolving-to-create-a-new-you.html

31 https://www.thelovepost.global/perspective/articles/collection-thought-provoking-quotes-stephen-hawking

Also by Jane Hutcheon

China Baby Love

From Rice to Riches

The Beijing Bureau (contributor)